Before They Were Famous

Nellie Bly

Written by Stephen Krensky
Illustrated by Bobbie Houser

A Crabtree Crown Book

CRABTREE
Publishing Company
www.crabtreebooks.com

School-to-Home Support for Caregivers and Teachers

This appealing book is designed to teach students about core subject areas. Students will build upon what they already know about the subject, and engage in topics that they want to learn more about. Here are a few guiding questions to help readers build their comprehension skills. Possible answers appear here in red.

Before Reading:

What do I know about this topic?
- I know that Nellie Bly was a female journalist.
- I know that Nellie Bly was a pen name and not the journalist's real name.

What do I want to learn about this topic?
- I want to learn what prompted Nellie to become an investigative journalist.
- I want to learn about Nellie Bly's trip around the world.

During Reading:

I'm curious to know…
- I'm curious to know why women in Nellie Bly's home city of Pittsburgh earned such a small amount of money each day.
- I wonder why Nellie Bly wasn't afraid to write articles about the horrors that were taking place in factories.

How is this like something I already know?
- I already knew that women did not receive the same pay as men in the 1800s.
- I knew that Nellie Bly later became famous for traveling around the world in 72 days.

After Reading:

What was the author trying to teach me?
- I think the author is trying to teach me about the hardships women in America encountered during the 1800s.
- I think the author is trying to teach me that there were always brave women who worked to change the terrible conditions women had to endure.

How did the photographs and captions help me understand more?
- The pictures of the steel mills in Pittsburgh with smoke pouring out made me realize that factories contributed much to air pollution.
- From the captions I learned that the newspapers in the United States can report the news without being controlled by the government, and that reporters are protected by the First Amendment.

Table of Contents

A Nervous Beginning 4
Getting Published 10
Going Undercover 14
A Mexican Adventure 22
Moving On 28
Glossary 30
Index 31
Comprehension Questions 31

A Nervous Beginning

Elizabeth Cochran was nervous. She was 20 years old, and she had never finished high school. Over the last four years, Pink, as her mother called her, had worked at one **dead-end** job after another.

Fun Facts

Nellie was known as Pink because when she was little, her mother always dressed her in pink dresses.

And yet here she was speaking with George Madden, the editor of the *Pittsburgh Dispatch* in Pittsburgh, Pennsylvania.

5

The newspaper had been running articles making fun of women for wanting to have careers.

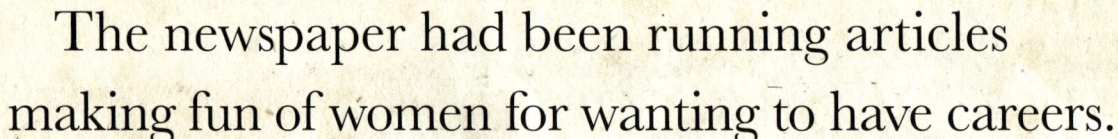

Many believed women should stay home and cook and clean.

Fun Facts

Although Nellie called herself Lonely Orphan Girl, she wasn't an orphan. Her father had died, but her mother was alive and well.

That kind of thinking had made Pink mad. So she had written a letter to the *Dispatch* telling them exactly what was wrong with their **old-fashioned** ideas. She had signed it, *Lonely Orphan Girl*.

Surprisingly, Mr. Madden liked her letter so much that he had wanted to meet her. And now that they were talking, he wanted to hire her to write an article about women in the business world.

Pink was surprised and delighted.

News

Pittsburgh, Pennsylvania during the late 1800s

Fun Facts

The *Pittsburgh Dispatch*, a leading newspaper in Pittsburgh, had been founded in 1846.

Getting Published

The article was published a week later. It explained about the awkward position women held in **society**. They might become teachers or clerks or chambermaids. But the only real way for them to get ahead was to get married.

This wasn't right, Pink had written. Women who had the ability should have the chance to prove themselves. "Pull them out of the **mire**," Pink wrote, "and give them a shove up the ladder of life."

DIVORCE

Pink then wrote another article, this one about divorce. She questioned many unhappy women about their relationships. It made her wonder about something many people accepted—that a bad marriage was better than no marriage at all.

Mr. Madden was now so pleased he offered Pink a full-time job. But what name should she use as a **byline** instead of *Lonely Orphan Girl*? Someone suggested Nelly Bly, a girl's name in a popular song. Pink was willing to try it, but the newspaper printer changed the spelling to Nellie Bly.

Fun Facts

"Nelly Bly" was a song about a servant written by Stephen Foster in 1850.

Stephen Foster

Going Undercover

And what was Nellie Bly going to write about? Well, she was curious about factories. Factories could be grimy and dangerous. Workers often worked twelve hours a day, six days a week.

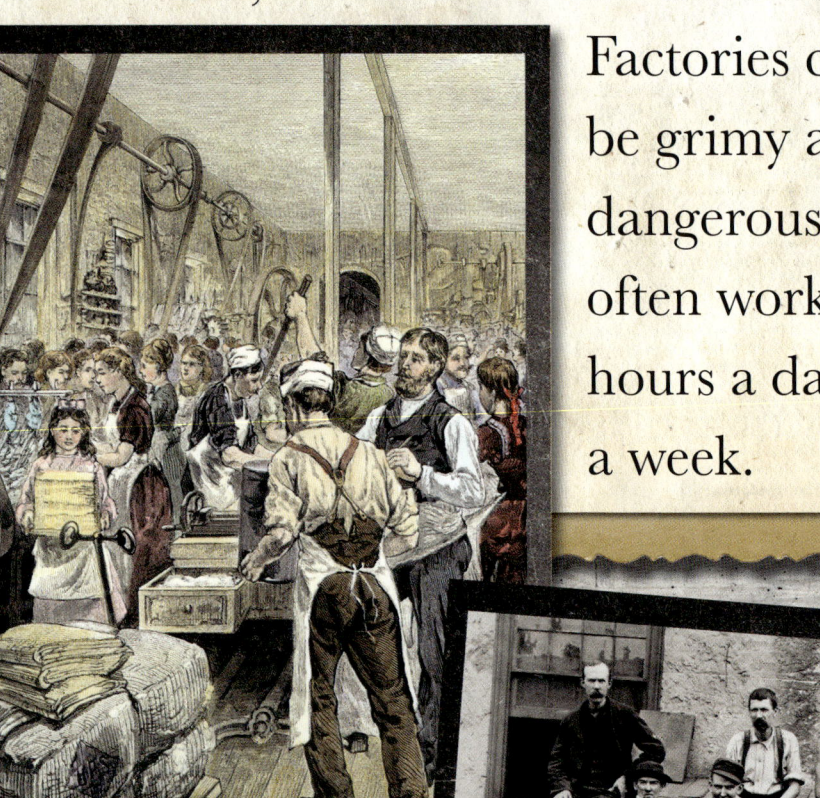

Many of these places had terrible **reputations**, but the rumors were hard to prove because the factory owners wouldn't let reporters inside for a look. What were they hiding?

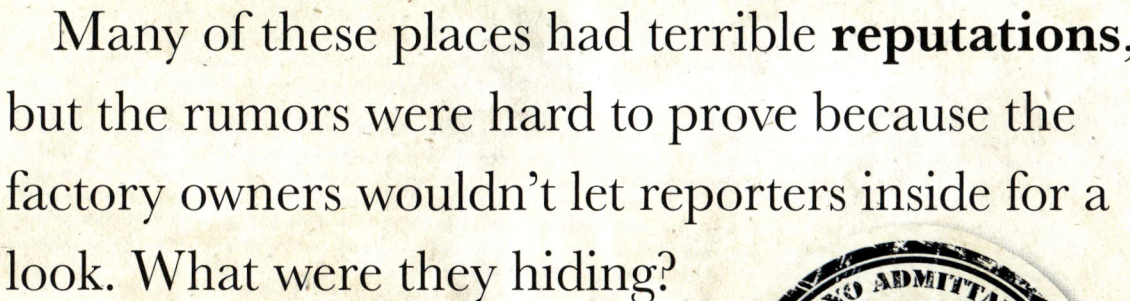

Steel mills darken the sky over Pittsburgh, Pennsylvania.

Fun Facts

The air in Pittsburgh, like many American cities of the time, was heavily polluted by the smoke coming out of factories.

Nellie decided to find out. She pretended to be unemployed and then found work in a basement workshop. Her job was to twist thin copper wires into thicker copper cables.

Twisting wires once or twice was easy. Twisting them all day long made her fingers sore and achy.

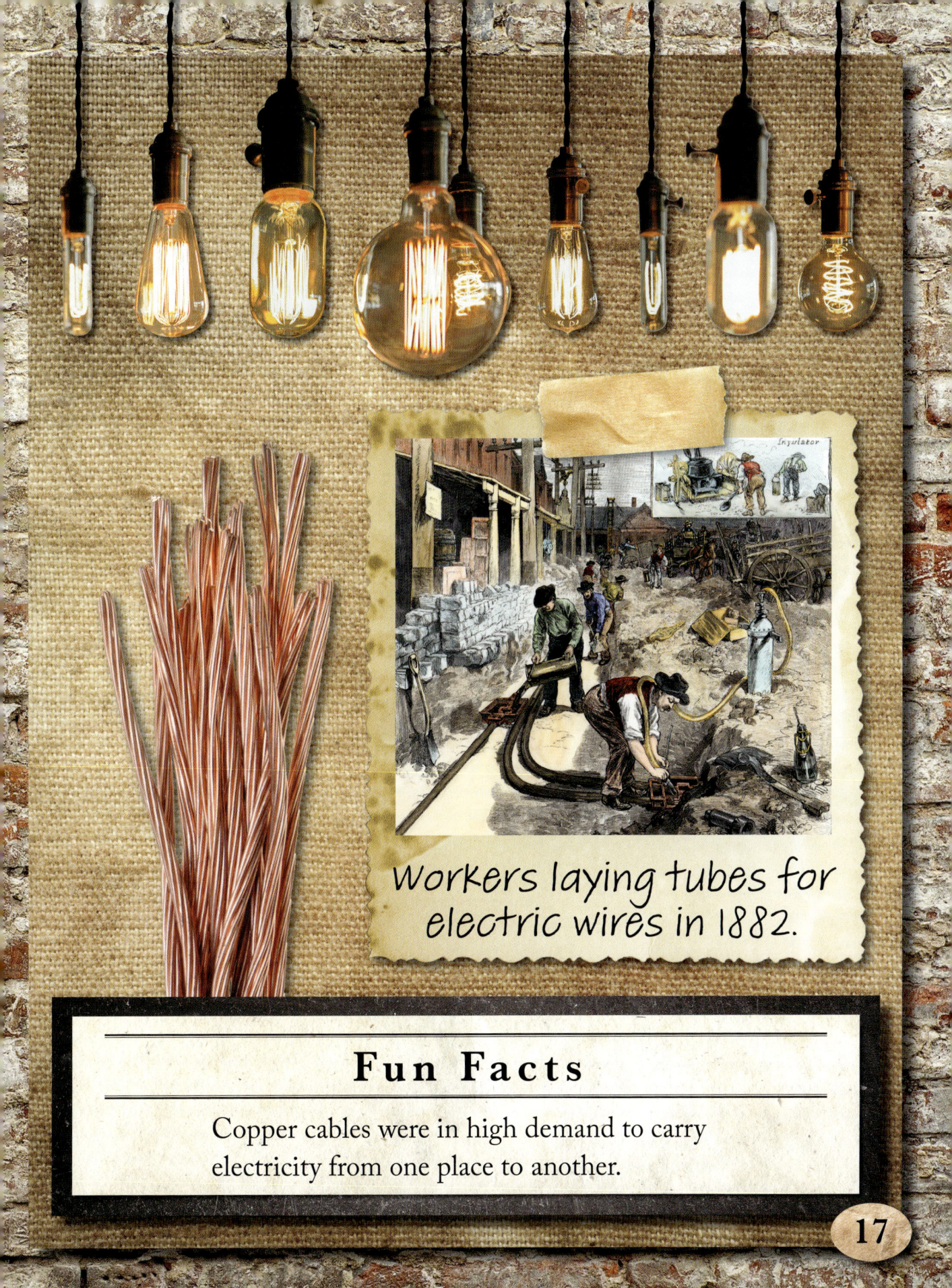

Workers laying tubes for electric wires in 1882.

Fun Facts

Copper cables were in high demand to carry electricity from one place to another.

It was dusty in the basement too. Soon Nellie was thirsty. But she couldn't even get a drink of water without getting permission first.

When Nellie wrote about her experience in the factory, her article captured the sadness many of the workers felt.

"I work hard all day, week after week for a mere **pittance**," she quoted one worker saying. "I go home at night tired of labor, and longing for something new, anything good or bad, to break the **monotony** of my existence."

NOTICE
STAY ON JOB TILL WHISTLE BLOWS

This kind of writing had never been seen in Pittsburgh before. It was raw and honest. As Nellie did more investigating, her work became well known around town.

Fun Facts

Nellie wrote a number of articles about factory workers as a series called "Our Workshop Girls."

And that made her a thorn in the side of the factory owners. The factory owners wanted to be left alone. They didn't want some girl reporter stirring up trouble. If the newspaper didn't make her stop, they would pull their **advertising**.

A Mexican Adventure

Facing this financial pressure, the *Dispatch* agreed to make a change. Nellie was asked to cover the events women reporters usually wrote about, things such as flower shows or society balls.

Nellie tried to fit in, but she couldn't do it. Instead, she suggested she go to Mexico. The editor reminded her that she didn't speak Spanish. And Mexico was known to be dangerous.

All the better, thought Nellie. She was ready for a real adventure.

Fun Facts

Nellie had met some officials from Mexico when they had visited Pittsburgh. They had invited her to come see them in Mexico.

23

In Mexico, Nellie spent almost six months writing about the lives and customs of the people she met.

Fun Facts

Nellie's mother went with her on the Mexico trip. At that time, it would not have been proper for Nellie, as a single woman, to travel alone.

But Nellie did more that just describe what she was seeing. When a local reporter was put in prison for disagreeing with the Mexican government, she wrote about that too.

The Mexican government was not pleased at all to hear about this report, and Nellie was threatened with arrest herself.

Clearly, it was time to go home.

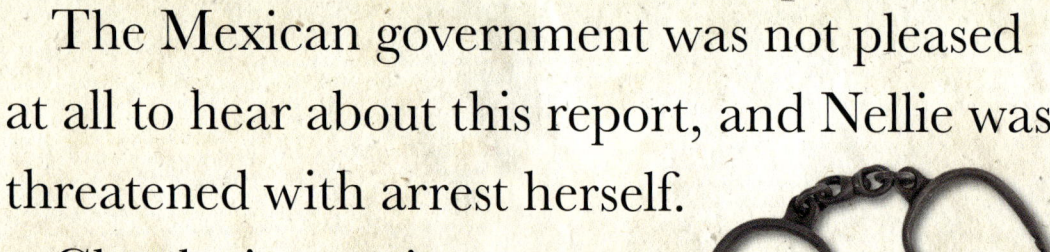

FREEDOM

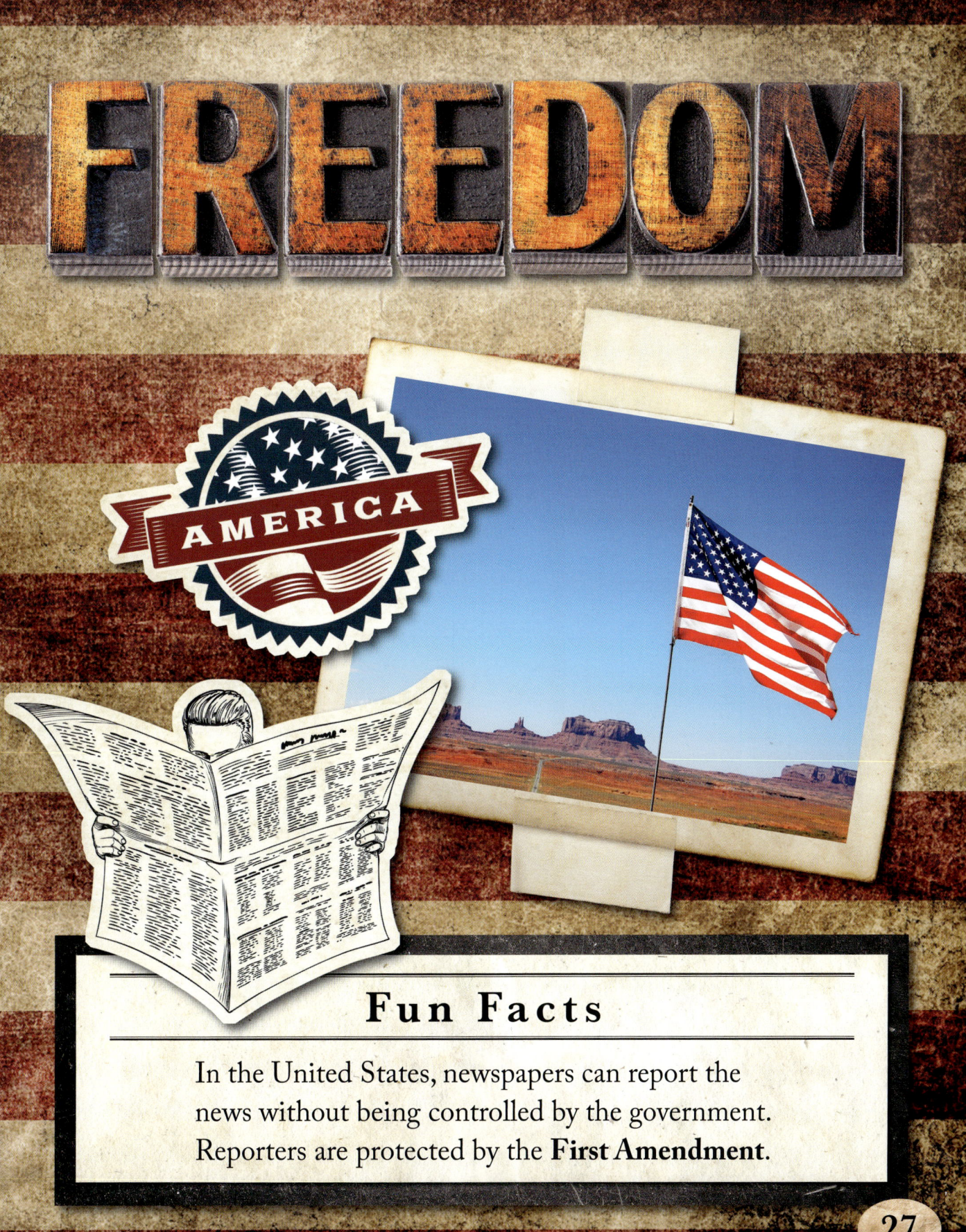

Fun Facts

In the United States, newspapers can report the news without being controlled by the government. Reporters are protected by the **First Amendment**.

Moving On

When Nellie got back, she wasn't sure if Pittsburgh had gotten smaller or she had gotten bigger. Either way, she didn't want to stay. There were bigger issues to cover and bigger places to cover them.

It was time for Nellie Bly to uncover them for herself.

Fun Facts

Nellie arrived in New York City in 1886. It took her a few months before she found work as a reporter.

    Nellie Bly was one of the first people, male or female, to go undercover to investigate wrongdoings and then write about them. She moved to New York after her time in Pittsburgh and got a job reporting for the New York World. Her most famous articles were written about the terrible conditions that existed in a local institution for women with mental illnesses. To expose these conditions, Nellie pretended to be struggling with her mental health, and then she lived in the institution for ten days. In a different kind of adventure, she later traveled around the world in 72 days, the fastest time ever up to that point.

    Nellie retired from reporting in 1895 and died at the age of 56 in 1922.

GLOSSARY

advertising
A written or visual announcement that promotes a service or product

byline
A line at the beginning of a newspaper or magazine article that gives the writer's name

dead-end
A position or path with no hope of advancement or way out beyond the current place

First Amendment
The First Amendment was part of the Bill of Rights that was added to the U.S. Constitution in 1791. It protects several basic freedoms, including freedom of speech and freedom of the press.

mire
Muddy ground or a sticky situation that a person will have trouble getting out of

monotony
The same situation repeated over and over again

old-fashioned
A viewpoint based on information or customs that are no longer current

pittance
A very small amount, usually of money

reputation
The common opinion that people have about something or someone

society
An established community of people, often with a strong sense of who is in charge

INDEX

factories   14, 15, 16, 18, 19, 20, 21

First Amendment   27

Foster, Stephen   13

Madden, George   5, 8, 13

Mexico   23, 24, 25, 26

"Nelly Bly"   13

New York City   28, 29

Pittsburgh Dispatch   5, 6, 7, 8, 9, 13, 20, 21, 22

COMPREHENSION QUESTIONS

How old was Nellie when she visited the offices of the *Pittsburgh Dispatch*?

What was Nellie's job in the factory?

Why did Nellie have to leave Mexico?

ABOUT THE AUTHOR

Stephen Krensky is the award-winning author of more than 150 fiction and nonfiction books for children. He and his wife Joan live in Lexington, Massachusetts, and he happily spends as much time as possible with his grown children and not-so-grown grandchildren.

Written by: Stephen Krensky
Illustrations by: Bobbie Houser
Art direction and layout by: Bobbie Houser
Series Development: James Earley
Proofreader: Petrice Custance
Educational Consultant: Marie Lemke M.Ed.
Print Coordinator: Katherine Berti

Photographs: t = Top, c = Center, b = Bottom, l = Left, r = Right
Alamy: Photo Researchers/ Science History Images: pp. 4 r, 28; Lakeview Images: p. 6 t; Patrick Guenette: p. 9 c; Science History Images: p. 13 c; North Wind Picture Archives: pp. 14 tl, 15 br, 17 r, 20 tl, br, 22 bl; H. ARMSTRONG ROBERTS/ClassicStock: pp. 14 br, 15 l; JT Vintage/Glasshouse Images: p. 19 b; SBS Eclectic Images: p. 29 tr; Shutterstock: AVA Bitter: cover tl, p. 25 tr; Everett Collection: cover bl, p. 29 b; Jaromond: cover br, p. 26 b; irina_angelic: p. 4 l; squarelogo: p. 5 t; Kseniakrop: p.5 b; Stuart Monk: p. 6 bl; alicedaniel: p. 6 br; DioGen: p. 7 t; vector punch: p. 7 r; Aquir: p. 8 t; magicoven: p. 8 b; enterlinedesign: p. 9 t; RetroClipArt: p. 9 b; Sabelskaya: p. 10 l; MaJaPa: p. 10 c; LiliGraphie: p. 10 r; Macrovector: p. 10 rb; ArtMari: pp. 11 tl, 20 cr; BrAt82: p. 11 tr; Nadya Dobrynina: p. 11 b; Marie Smolej: p. 12 t; Emir Simsek: p. 12 l; Paul Orr: p. 12 r; dinvector: p. 13 l, r; Jeanne McRight: p. 14 bl; MichaelJayBerlin: p. 15 tr; vectorfusionart: p. 16 t; Prostock-studio: p. 16 b; Ezume Images: p. 17 t; Flegere: p. 17 l; ducu59us: p. 18; Anetlanda: p. 19 t; di Bronzino: p. 19 c; Torsten Lorenz: p. 20 tr; SNeG17: p. 21 l; Astarina: p. 21 r; rraya: p. 22 t; Francesco Milanese: p. 23 tr; Malakhova Iryna: p. 23 cr; Pablo Caridad: p. 23 bl; aksol: pp. 23 br, 24 b; SkyPics Studio: p. 24 t; rustamank: p. 25 tl; TatianaKost94: p. 25 bl; Pictrider: p. 25 br; David Orcea: p. 26 t; marekuliasz: p. 27 t; Oleg Iatsun: p. 27 cl; Stefania Rossitto: p. 27 r; Marzufello: p. 27 bl; Bukhavets Mikhail: p. 29 tl

Library and Archives Canada Cataloguing in Publication

Available at the Library and Archives Canada

Library of Congress Cataloging-in-Publication Data

Available at the Library of Congress

Crabtree Publishing Company
www.crabtreebooks.com   1-800-387-7650

Copyright © 2023 **CRABTREE PUBLISHING COMPANY**

All rights reserved. No part of this publication may be reproduced, stored in a retrieval system or be transmitted in any form or by any means, electronic, mechanical, photocopying, recording, or otherwise, without the prior written permission of Crabtree Publishing Company. In Canada: We acknowledge the financial support of the Government of Canada through the Canada Book Fund for our publishing activities.

Published in the United States
Crabtree Publishing
347 Fifth Avenue
Suite 1402-145
New York, NY, 10016

Published in Canada
Crabtree Publishing
616 Welland Ave.
St. Catharines, ON
L2M 5V6

Printed in the U.S.A./072022/CG20220201